4th

TRITON ELEMENTARY LIBRARY
TRITON SCHOOL CORPORATION
BOURBON, INDIANA

REACHING FOR THE STARS

PAULA ABDUL
Choreographer, Dancer, Singer

Written by: Sue L. Hamilton

Published by Abdo & Daughters, 6535 Cecilia Circle, Edina, Minnesota 55439

Library bound edition distributed by Rockbottom Books, Pentagon Tower, P.O. Box 36036, Minneapolis, Minnesota 55435

Copyright© 1990 by Abdo Consulting Group, Inc., Pentagon Tower, P.O. Box 36036, Minneapolis, Minnesota 55435. International copyrights reserved in all countries. No part of this book may be reproduced in any form without written permission from the publisher. Printed in the United States.

Library of Congress Number: 90-083611   ISBN: 1-56239-012-0

Cover Illustrations by: Retna Ltd.
Inside Photos by: Retna Ltd.

Edited by: Rosemary Wallner

TABLE OF CONTENTS

A Hot New Talent 5

Learning to Dance 7

New Ideas 11

The Laker Girls 13

Music Videos, Movies and Commercials 15

A Pop Singer 21

Continuing Her Success 29

Paula Abdul's Address 32

Paula Abdul — The hottest new talent in the music industry.

A HOT NEW TALENT

TVs across the United States flicker with the pictures and sounds of popular music videos. Musicians incorporate their songs into these miniature movies ranging from the wild and strange to the simple and tame. But one young woman's unique style has come to stand out above the rest.

With the release of her very first album, *Forever Your Girl,* four of Paula Abdul's songs ("Straight Up," "Forever Your Girl," "Cold Hearted," and "Opposites Attract") have gone to Number 1 on both music and music video charts. The album itself has gone quadruple-platinum — meaning it has sold over 8 million copies. In only a few years, Paula Abdul has become one of the hottest new talents in the music industry. But her amazing popularity did not happen overnight. It has taken work. Lots of it.

Paula combines tap, jazz, and ballet together to make dance moves like no one else.

LEARNING TO DANCE

"If you really believe in yourself and work hard, somehow, some way, things will happen for you!" said Abdul in a recent interview. Hard work does make a difference, but talent also plays a big part in success. And Paula Abdul certainly has plenty of that.

Terms such as "street-smart" and "funky-street" dancing have been used to describe Abdul's distinctive dance style. Abdul combines tap, jazz, and ballet and blend's them together to make her moves like no one else's. And it is a style that Abdul has been developing since she was a kid.

Born on June 19, 1962, Paula Julie Abdul grew up in a middle-class neighborhood in North Hollywood, California. Her unique looks are a combination of her father's Syrian and Brazilian background and her mother's French-Canadian Jewish descent. Abdul's father, Harry, worked as a cattle rancher. Her mother, Lorraine, worked as an assistant to a director at a nearby film studio. It was her mother's job that first introduced Abdul to the entertainment scene. Stated Abdul, "What's funny is going back to the studios for meetings. Some of the same guards are there, and they still remember me as Lorraine's daughter."

Everyone faces some difficulties in life, and Abdul was no exception. When she was seven years old, her parents divorced. Abdul went to live with her mother and sister, Wendy. Her sister, who is seven years older, introduced Abdul to a wide variety of music. "Most of the kids around were into Shaun Cassidy and the DeFranco Family," said Abdul. "But I also heard all the music Wendy and her hippie friends listened to — Joni Mitchell, Stevie Wonder, Carole King, and Iron Butterfly."

Abdul listened to the music and watched her sister's older friends, and soon developed an interest in dance. By chance, she walked by a dance studio on her way to grade school each day. Before long, she was inside, learning everything she could. "Dancing — ballet, tap, jazz — was like a reward to me. A special treat," explained Abdul.

At eight years old she was already dancing and performing. Abdul made up dance routines for herself and her friends at home and at school, including an early routine for The Archies "Sugar, Sugar." For Abdul, arranging dance steps was fun. And her talent was obvious, not only to family members and friends, but to school teachers and officials, as well. "I'd get involved in school shows — acting or singing — then they'd find out about my dancing," laughed Abdul. "Then they would ask, 'Well, can you set up a routine for the kids?' 'Sure' I'd say. No one ever minded."

Abdul kept working on her own dancing and by the time she was in sixth grade, she had choreographed (created dance steps and movements for) her first musical, *Hello Dolly!*

Friendly and outgoing, Paula is always ready for a new challenge.

NEW IDEAS

Abdul entered Van Nuys High School with a string of dancing successes already behind her. Friendly and outgoing, the attractive girl was ready for new challenges. Not only did she continue to work on school plays, but she was also a Student Council member, flutist in the school orchestra, a member of the science team, senior class president, and head cheerleader.

In a recent interview, Abdul recalled her cheerleading routines, "Cheerleading was so traditional, with the pompons and the cheers. I felt, okay, let's do that but do some dance routines, too, so I started changing the whole style of cheerleading. The teams were getting more involved because they really liked the dance steps."

"I found out early on that if something was too hard it wouldn't look good," said Abdul. "It's always great to extend yourself, but sometimes the easier movement looks the most effective. In working with any group, your whole team is only as good as the weakest person on the squad." And Paula knew how to make her cheerleading team look good . . . but in her own way.

Known for breaking tradition, she set up routines that did not use pompons. She brought in the music that she thought worked. "I would take a boom-box and put it up to the microphone and just forget about the band that was playing really dorky music," admitted Abdul.

Clearly Abdul had her own ideas on how to choreograph. Her opportunities and experiences in high school set her up for her next big step into success.

THE LAKER GIRLS

After high school, Abdul decided to go on to college. Her short height kept her from her dreams of becoming a professional dancer. Instead, Abdul enrolled in California State University, Northridge, majoring in sportscasting.

Seeking a part-time job, she decided to try out for a cheerleading job with the local professional basketball team — the Los Angeles Lakers. Being a "Laker Girl" combined two of her favorite things: sports and dance. The job also gave her an opportunity to earn some spending money. Besides, she hoped to interview some of the basketball players for her college work.

But when the young eighteen-year-old Abdul went to audition, she almost did not go in. ". . . I got down to the tryout and there were hundreds of tall, beautiful girls there," said Abdul, "I said to myself, 'I'm not going to do this.'" But bolstering her courage, she went ahead with the one-minute routine she had prepared. The judges liked her style and asked her to join the squad.

Those sixty seconds had changed her life forever. "It was like that big moment at the end of *Flashdance,* when Jennifer Beals struts her stuff," remembered Abdul. A few months later Abdul became the squad's choreographer. Under her direction, the Laker Girls soon developed new routines and movements. Before long, Abdul transformed the Lakers basketball players and Laker Girls cheerleaders into the Number 1 sports and entertainment team. People came not only to watch their favorite basketball team play, but also to watch the Laker Girls perform.

Abdul knew how to make the routines look good, and was given the freedom to do her job as she thought best. Not only could she create the unique dances and movements, but she worked with the camera crews to be sure the Laker Girls looked good on TV. "Any time a routine was being shown," stated Abdul, "I was able to work with the camera crews and tell them to get a wide angle shot of this or that. I would have the girls work in different formations, just so the (TV) crew could get used to it . . ." Abdul left nothing to chance, and kept watching and learning. At the same time, her skills were being noticed by more than just the regular Lakers fans.

MUSIC VIDEOS, MOVIES AND COMMERCIALS

Many people from the entertainment industry were Lakers fans. The Jacksons, the popular singing family, were season-ticket holders. The family frequently saw and admired Abdul's work with the Laker Girls. In 1984, Abdul was asked to choreograph Janet Jackson's first video, *Torture*.

For the next year, Abdul worked closely with Jackson, getting to know her and finding out what the singer wanted. Abdul listened and, given "one hundred percent freedom of style," created a dance style that showed Jackson "sassy and in control."

In 1987, Jackson won the 1987 MTV Choreography Award. Abdul was asked to work *only* for Jackson's A&M music label. Although Abdul and Jackson had become "like sisters," Abdul turned down the offer. She wanted to remain independent.

The entertainment industry found Abdul's unique dance style hot. She soon found herself working with a variety of top singing stars: George Michael, Prince, ZZ Top, the Pointer Sisters, Steve Winwood, Dolly Parton, Debbie Gibson and Warren Zevon. But her talents did not stop there.

She was also asked to help choreograph scenes in movies. She worked with Arnold Schwarzenegger in *Running Man*; with Dan Aykroyd and Tom Hanks in the video clip for *Dragnet*; created the African dance number in Eddie Murphy's movie *Coming to America*; and dance scenes on "The Tracey Ullman Show" (which lead to an Emmy Award nomination.)

Each job brought out new challenges for the young choreographer. Some people were easy to teach. Others were not. But Paula had her own way of making everything work out. "For singers and actors with limited dance abilities, I need to design a concept. I give them ideas of a character to portray. I bring out the best in them by digging it out," said Abdul. "I like to do the feature films, which can take from one to three months, because you get to know the talent and grow with them to create something special."

Paula seen here with Christy Brinkley and Billy Joel.

Advertising professionals also saw the popularity and modern style Abdul created. So she entered this business and faced some new challenges. Instead of featuring a person's movements, she now had to get a person to feature a product.

Said Abdul, "Choreographing commercials is very hard because they are only thirty-second spots . . . and you know that whatever dance is ultimately seen will last only a split second. You have to work such long hours to get that one second."

With commercials you also have the director, production crew, and client making sure the product is seen. All the dance for the Nissan (car) commercial, for example, had to be choreographed around the rearview and side view mirrors. "Sometimes it's frustrating because you think 'I'm going to capture the greatest dance move there,'" said Abdul, "and when you finally see it you don't really have that much."

Once, again, however, Abdul took over, learned, and did her best. Yet, for all her challenges, successes, and popularity, the young star wanted something more. During a ZZ Top video shoot, she approached Jess Ayeroff, a music business professional. She told him she wanted to make records. She gave him a tape of a song she had recorded with two other Laker Girls. The tape was enough to convince Ayeroff and his associate, Jordan Harris, that she should be given the opportunity to cut a real eight-track audition tape.

It was a step toward stardom.

Paula works very hard to create unique dance steps.

With her new album, Paula Abdul was able to choreograph dance moves to her songs.

A POP SINGER

Abdul signed with Virgin Records and began recording her first album *Forever Your Girl,* as hopeful as any new singer that it would be a success. The album became a smash hit, whirling the attractive dancer/choreographer into the realm of pop singer.

From there came the music videos, where, for the first time as a professional, she created her own dances to perform with her own songs. Clearly, music and video fans across the country loved her style. Her fame sent her album, four individual songs (known as "singles"), and the videos from those singles straight to the top of the charts.

Paula working on a video.

Her singing and dancing were just the right combination. Said Abdul, "The thing I love about dancing is that I'm able to express myself through my body — my style comes right from my heart with sharp, quick, very articulate movements. And with singing I can really express my emotions."

Abdul's individual style has made a strong impact all across the United States. One of her old jazz and tap instructors, Dean Barlow, who still runs a dance studio in Hollywood, often gets calls from kids who want him to teach them to dance "Paula Abdul style." And Paula could not be happier. She stated, "Kids place a lot of importance on dance these days. Instead of games and sports, kids are getting into dance-offs. Dance is no longer a spectator sport."

Has success changed her? In some ways, her life had to change. Before, she was well-known in the entertainment industry. Now she is recognized all over the country. In other ways, however, she has remained the same. Her favorite song on the album, "It's Just (the Way That You Love Me)," expresses a lot about the friendly, young professional. "It's a fun song," stated Abdul. "It says that I'm not impressed with material things. It tells a guy he doesn't have to have a nice car or tons of money."

But once you have had such a great success, what is next?

Her next album is in the works. Most of her past songs have been written by professional songwriters (although "Forever Your Girl" has some lines that Abdul wrote). For this album, she plans to write several of her own songs. Yet another job for the busy entertainer.

And what does someone so busy do for fun? Does she take time out for dates and movies?

Paula with actor John Stamos.

Rumors have spread fast and furious that she and talk show host/actor Arsenio Hall have a close relationship. Although Abdul admitted that someday she would like to get married and start a family, right now there just is no time. And as for Arsenio, she said that he is "the man I'm closest with and someone who I can talk to about everything I'm going through, because he's going through it, too."

Stated Hall in a recent interview, "We're good friends. And being a good friend means a lot of things to me. I'm her brother when someone's bugging her. I'm her buddy when she needs to go to a movie. When she's sad and sheds a few tears, I'm a shoulder. I put my arms around her and comfort her. I talk with her forever on the phone when she calls in the middle of the night. I'm everything a good friend needs to be. We're close. *Very* close."

Paula's success hasn't slowed her down. She still moves at a fast pace.

CONTINUING HER SUCCESS

The 1980's were an amazing whirlwind for the young star. Can she continue the fast-paced success?

Abdul admitted that "it's hard to stay fresh." She videotapes herself once a week to discover new movements. But the young performer knows that she loves dancing and singing, and that she wants to keep doing more.

"I love being in front of the camera and behind it," said Abdul. "I want to be an all-around entertainer. When people see you, they are touched in a way that they can't be just from hearing your record. I want to leave a visual impression with people so that when I perform, they'll say, 'Wow! Did you see Paula Abdul?'"

Abdul has worked hard to get where she is at. She is not afraid to work hard in the future. Although her challenge will be to stay on top (not an easy thing to do in the entertainment industry), for right now, she is already there. And as Abdul admitted when thinking of her success: "I'm just very, *very* happy."

PAULA ABDUL'S ADDRESS

You can write to Paula Abdul at:

Paula Abdul
c/o Platinum Management
1244 Wilshire Boulevard
Los Angeles, CA 90025

TRITON ELEMENTARY LIBRARY
TRITON SCHOOL CORPORATION
BOURBON, INDIANA

DATE DUE			
DEC 12 1990	SEP 11 1991	JAN 6 1992	SEP 8 '92
DEC 20 1990	SEP 30 1991	JAN 28 1992	SEP 17 '92
JAN 2 1991	OCT 7 1991	FEB 11 1992	SEP 24 '92
JAN 21 1991	OCT 14 1991	FEB 18 1992	MAY 21 '93
JAN 29 1991	OCT 22 1991	MAR 3 1992	
		MAR 9 1992	
FEB 12 1991	OCT 31 1991	MAR 19 1992	
APR 31 1991	NOV 20 1991	MAR 26 1992	
MAY 9 1991	NOV 27 1991	APR 6 1992	
MAY 10 1991	DEC 6 1991	APR 20 1992	
MAY 17 1991		APR 29 1992	
MAY 24 1991	DEC 19 1991	MAY 7 1992	
SEP 3 1991	DEC 20 1991	MAY 21 '92	

4th   90247

```
784       Hamilton, Sue.
HAM         Paula Abdul /
 C-1       singing sensation.
```

Reaching for the Stars, Series